Solar System Explorers

Pluto and Other Dwarf Planets

Written by
Charis Mather

KidHaven PUBLISHING

Published in 2026 by
KidHaven Publishing, an Imprint of
Greenhaven Publishing, LLC
2544 Clinton St., Buffalo, NY 14224

Written by: Charis Mather
Edited by: Noah Leatherland
Designed by: Amelia Harris

All facts, statistics, web addresses, and URLs in this book were verified as valid and accurate at time of writing. No responsibility for any changes to external websites or references can be accepted by either the author or publisher.

Cataloging-in-Publication Data
Names: Mather, Charis.
Title: Pluto and other dwarf planets / Charis Mather.
Description: Buffalo, NY : Kidhaven Publishing, 2026. | Series: Solar System Explorers | Includes glossary and index
Identifiers: ISBN 9781534551466 (pbk) | ISBN 9781534551473 (library bound) | ISBN 9781534551480 (ebook)
Subjects: LCSH: Ceres (Dwarf planet)—Juvenile Literature | Dwarf Planets—Juvenile Literature | Pluto (Dwarf planet)—Juvenile Literature
Classification: LCC QB698 M38 2026 | DDC 523.49--dc25

Manufactured in the United States of America

CPSIA compliance information: Batch #CSKH26
For further information contact Greenhaven Publishing LLC
at 1-844-317-7404.

Image Credits

Images are courtesy of Shutterstock.com. With thanks to Getty Images, Thinkstock Photo and iStockphoto. Cover – AspctStyle, andreysharonov, NASA images, diluck, Yurij Omelchenko. Recurring Images – thomas eder, YummyBuum, Sabelskaya. 4–5 – Nostalgia for Infinity, ESA (acknowledgement: work performed by ATG under contract to ESA), CC BY-SA IGO 3.0, CC BY-SA 3.0 IGO via Wikimedia Commons. 6–7 – BreizhAtao, Chawalit Banpot. 8–9 – Zonda, SN VFX, Diego Barucco. 10–11 – Daniil Disa, NASA, ESA, and A. Feild (STScI), Public domain, via Wikimedia Commons, NASA, ESA, and A. Feild (STScI), Public domain, via Wikimedia Commons. 12–13 – 24K-Production, muratart, Jurik Peter, NASA/Johns Hopkins University Applied Physics Laboratory/Southwest Research Institute, Public domain, via Wikimedia Commons. 14–15 – OverAnimated, Diego Barucco. 16–17 – ESO/L. Calçada/Nick Risinger, CC BY 4.0 via Wikimedia Commons, jdrmkci. 18–19 – vectortatu, BreizhAtao, Evannovostro. 20–21 – Vadim Sadovski, Diego Barucco, joshimerbin, ESO/L. Calçada and Nick Risinger, CC BY 4.0 via Wikimedia Commons. 22–23 – Artsiom P.

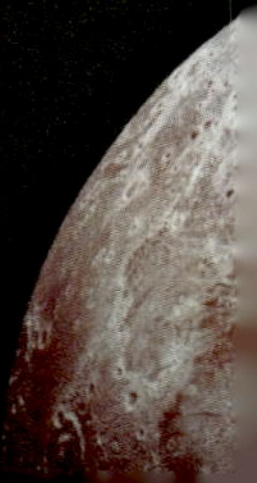

Contents

Words that look like this can be found in the glossary on page 24.

Let's Explore!

Have you ever heard of the solar system? The solar system is everything in space that **orbits** the sun. There are planets, moons, and dwarf planets. We want to explore every single one!

The sun is the biggest object in the solar system. Next biggest are planets. Dwarf planets and moons are even smaller. After that are rocky objects, called asteroids, that also orbit the sun.

What Are Dwarf Planets?

Dwarf planets are similar to normal planets in two ways. They are mostly round and orbit the sun. However, one important difference is that dwarf planets are smaller than other planets.

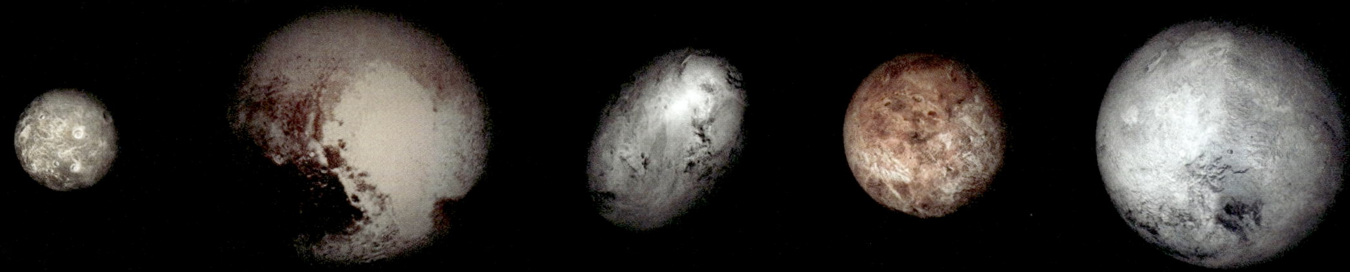

The dwarf planets are called Ceres, Pluto, Haumea, Makemake, and Eris.

Being smaller means that dwarf planets have weaker **gravity**. That means that unlike bigger planets with strong gravity, dwarf planets cannot keep the area around them clear of smaller space objects, such as asteroids.

Where Are The Dwarf Planets?

Most of the dwarf planets are very far out in the solar system. Most of them orbit the sun beyond the eight planets, in an enormous ring of asteroids called the Kuiper Belt.

Just one of the five dwarf planets we know of orbits closer to the sun. Ceres is part of a ring of asteroids called the asteroid belt. This belt orbits the sun between Mars and Jupiter.

Ceres

The outer layer of Ceres is covered in rock, dust, and **salts**. Underneath that, Ceres has a thick layer of icy material. Sometimes, that icy material bursts up from below, like frozen **volcanoes**.

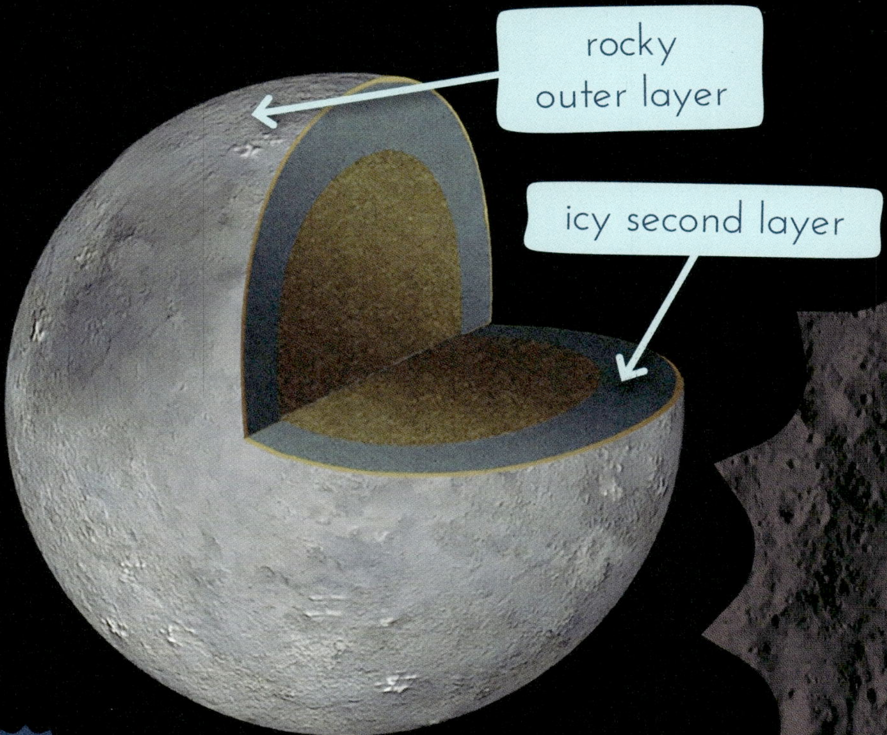

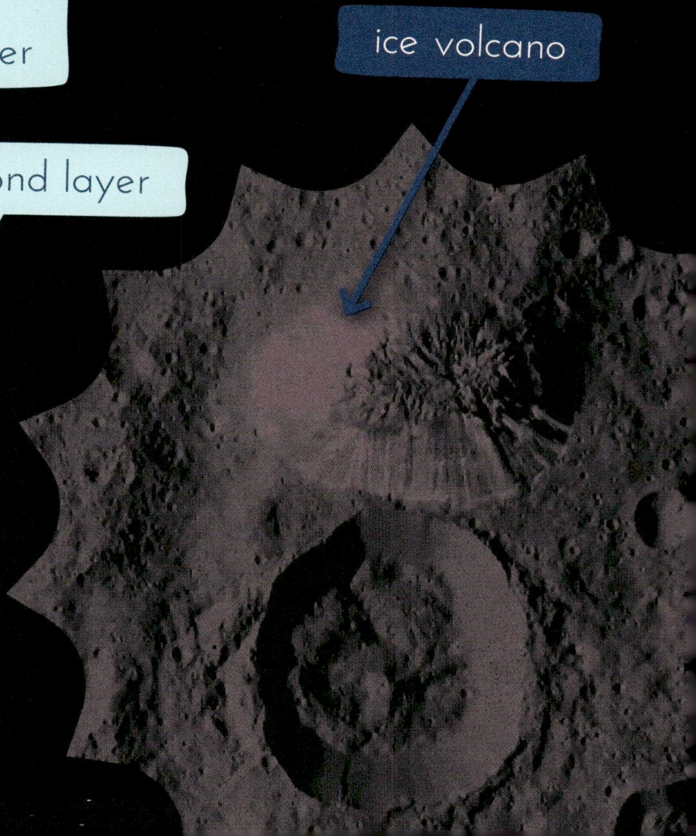

One day on Ceres only takes nine hours. However, a year takes more than four and a half Earth years. This is because of how far Ceres has to travel to orbit the sun once.

A day is how long it takes a planet or dwarf planet to spin around once.

Pluto

Pluto is the solar system's largest dwarf planet. However, it is still smaller than Earth's moon. It takes about 153 hours for Pluto to spin once. It takes about 248 years to orbit the sun.

Pluto's rocky **surface** is covered in different kinds of ice and frost. The flat heart-shaped area is made of nitrogen ice. In other places, Pluto has mountains of frozen water and **gas**.

Haumea

Haumea stands out among the dwarf planets. Instead of having a round shape like the rest, Haumea is almost egg-shaped. This is because of how fast Haumea spins.

Haumea spins once every four hours. This makes it one of the solar system's fastest-spinning large objects. Although a day on Haumea is extremely short, a year takes nearly 285 Earth years.

Haumea is the solar system's only dwarf planet known to have a ring.

Makemake

Makemake is very far away from Earth, and that makes it hard to see. Even so, scientists have worked out that it is probably covered in frozen methane and ethane gas. This gives Makemake its reddish-brown color.

Makemake spins once about every 22 and a half hours. However, Makemake takes 305 Earth years to travel around the sun. That means that there are over 118 thousand Makemake days in a Makemake year.

Eris

On Eris, a day lasts 26 hours. This is similar to Earth's 24-hour days. However, a year on Eris takes 557 days. This is much longer than Earth's year, which takes 365 days.

Eris takes an oval-shaped path around the sun.

Sometimes, Eris travels so far from the sun that its **atmosphere** is unable to stay up. When Eris gets too cold, its atmosphere freezes. It falls onto the rocky dwarf planet as snow.

Spot the Satellites

Some of the dwarf planets have their own moons or chunks of rock that travel around them. These smaller orbiting objects are known as satellites.

Pluto

Pluto's moons are called Charon, Styx, Nix, Kerberos, and Hydra.

Eris

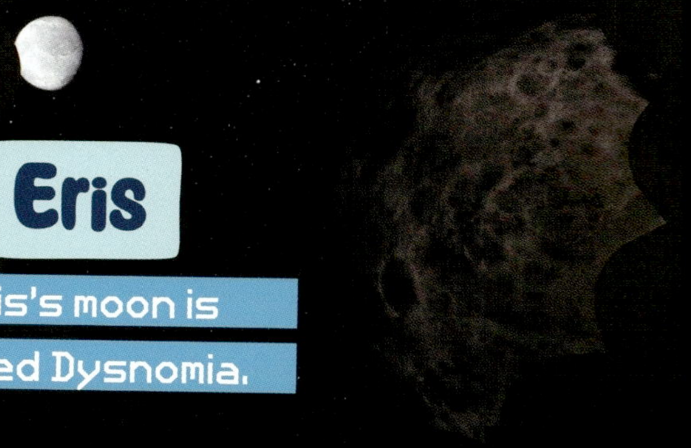

Eris's moon is called Dysnomia.

Haumea

Haumea's moons are called Namaka and Hi'iaka.

Ceres

Ceres has no moons, but it once had a human-made satellite called the Dawn spacecraft.

Makemake

Makemake has a moon that is known as MK 2.

More to Explore

Dwarf planets might not count as proper planets, but that does not make them any less interesting. Hopefully, we will be able to find out much more about these distant objects in the future.

For now, though, it is time to leave Ceres, Pluto, Haumea, Makemake, and Eris behind. We have a great big solar system to explore. There is always more to see!

Glossary

atmosphere the mixture of gases that makes up the air and surroundings

gas a thing that is like air, which fills any space available

gravity the force that pulls everything downward toward the center of large objects in space

orbits travels around a star or planet in a curved path

salts substances that are made when certain chemicals combine

surface the top or outer layer of something

volcanoes large mountains that sometimes erupt, giving off gases and other materials

Index

Solar System Explorers

Titles in This Series

Earth
Jupiter
Mars
Mercury
Neptune
Pluto and Other Dwarf Planets
Saturn
Uranus
Venus

ISBN: 9781534551466
9 781534 551466

KidHaven Publishing

COOL CHARACTERS

Write On!

Charis Mather